HEAD-TO-HEAD
LEGENDS

BY JAKE BLACK

■SCHOLASTIC

an imprint of
SCHOLASTIC
www.scholastic.com

Published by Tangerine Press,
an imprint of Scholastic Inc.,
557 Broadway, New York, NY 10012
Scholastic Canada Ltd., Markham, Ontario

becker&mayer!
BOOK PRODUCERS

WWE Head-to-Head: Legends
is produced by becker&mayer! LLC
11120 NE 33rd Place, Suite 101
Bellevue, WA 98004
www.beckermayer.com

Published by arrangement with Grosset & Dunlap,
a division of Penguin Young Readers Group,
a member of Penguin Group [USA] Inc.

If you have questions or comments about this product, please visit www.beckermayer.com/customerservice and click on Customer Service Request Form.

Author: Jake Black
Editors: Betsy Henry Pringle and Leah Jenness
Designer: Sam Dawson
Production coordinator: Tom Miller
Photo researcher: Katie del Rosario and Emily Zach
Managing editor: Nicole Burns Ascue

345190 6/13
Printed in Jefferson City, MO USA
10 9 8 7 6 5 4 3 2 1
ISBN: 978-0-545-58467-8
12670

Elements used throughout, all from Shutterstock.com unless otherwise credited: Abstract burst © Igor Zh.; Abstract explosion © Igor Zh.; Red fist © Sweet Lana; Wire fencing © Rakic; Barb wire © Gwoeii; Office icons © VooDooDotk; Cracked stone texture © Merkushev; Black cracks stone © kickdrum; Crowd silhouettes © Seyyahil; Old metal texture © NickSorl; Metal background © Phiseksit.

WWE HEAD-TO-HEAD
LEGENDS

The greatest WWE Superstars are going head-to-head with some of the best WWE Legends of all time. In each bruising matchup, you'll see all the stats and information you need to pick the winner. Turn to page 64 to see our experts' picks and who won the match!

THE MATCHUPS

WWE Championship

For fifty years, the WWE Championship has been the most prestigious championship in all of sports entertainment. Many legendary warriors like The Rock, Undertaker, Shawn Michaels, Triple H, John Cena, and CM Punk have held the title. When a Superstar wins the WWE Championship, he is universally considered to be the greatest in-ring competitor in the world. The first WWE Champion was "Nature Boy" Buddy Rogers, who won the title in 1963. Since then, just over forty Superstars have added their names to the elite list of champions.

CM PUNK vs. STONE COLD STEVE AUSTIN

CM Punk and Stone Cold Steve Austin are two of the fiercest fighters to ever set foot in a WWE ring. But that's about the only thing they have in common. Punk is "straight edge" so he doesn't drink, smoke, or use drugs. Austin is as fearless as he is tough. Both are talented Superstars. This clash will be intense!

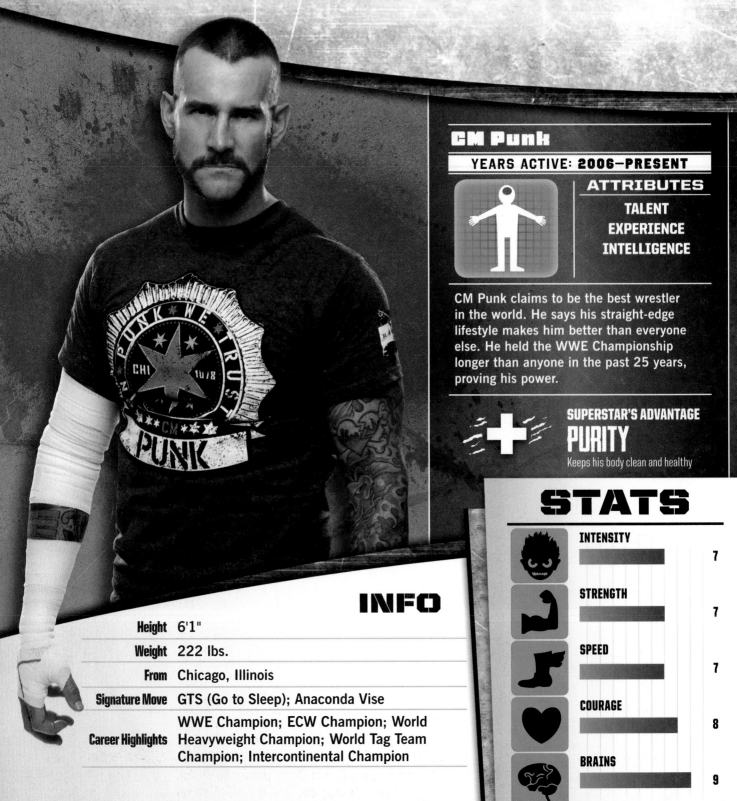

CM Punk

YEARS ACTIVE: 2006–PRESENT

ATTRIBUTES

TALENT
EXPERIENCE
INTELLIGENCE

CM Punk claims to be the best wrestler in the world. He says his straight-edge lifestyle makes him better than everyone else. He held the WWE Championship longer than anyone in the past 25 years, proving his power.

SUPERSTAR'S ADVANTAGE

PURITY

Keeps his body clean and healthy

INFO

Height	6'1"
Weight	222 lbs.
From	Chicago, Illinois
Signature Move	GTS (Go to Sleep); Anaconda Vise
Career Highlights	WWE Champion; ECW Champion; World Heavyweight Champion; World Tag Team Champion; Intercontinental Champion

STATS

INTENSITY		7
STRENGTH		7
SPEED		7
COURAGE		8
BRAINS		9

THE SHOWDOWN

Austin and Punk want to get at each other so badly that they don't wait for the opening bell. They exchange a series of blows, with neither one giving any advantage to the other. The referee tries to pull them apart long enough for the ring introductions, but they won't have it. They charge back at each other, pounding away.

Stone Cold Steve Austin

YEARS ACTIVE: 1991–2004

ATTRIBUTES
INTENSITY
DETERMINATION
POWER

Stone Cold Steve Austin is the most popular and successful Superstar in WWE history. In the 1990s, he fought the chairman of WWE, Mr. McMahon, and in doing so represented people everywhere who had a bone to pick with their boss.

LEGEND'S ADVANTAGE
FEARLESSNESS
Nothing scares him

STATS

INTENSITY		9
STRENGTH		8
SPEED		7
COURAGE		9
BRAINS		8

INFO

6'2"	Height
252 lbs.	Weight
Victoria, Texas	From
Stone Cold Stunner	Signature Move
WWE Champion; Intercontinental Champion; World Tag Team Champion; King of the Ring (1996); *Royal Rumble* Winner (1997, 1998, 2001); United States Champion; WCW Tag Team Champion; WWE Hall of Fame	Career Highlights

For the past decade, John Cena has been the face of WWE. He's won numerous championships and gained millions of fans. But looming in the shadows has been Undertaker. For nearly a quarter of a century, Undertaker has been the most powerful and most intimidating Superstar in WWE—and he has proven his power by his unprecedented undefeated 20-match *WrestleMania* streak.

John Cena

YEARS ACTIVE: 2002–PRESENT

ATTRIBUTES

HUSTLE
LOYALTY
RESPECT

John Cena believes hustle, loyalty, and respect are not only good ideas, they are a way of life. He never gives up and always fights for his beliefs—and his fans—against some of the WWE's most wicked warriors.

SUPERSTAR'S ADVANTAGE
MAN OF THE PEOPLE

INFO

Height	6'1"
Weight	240 lbs.
From	West Newbury, Massachusetts
Signature Move	Attitude Adjustment; STF
Career Highlights	World Heavyweight Champion; WWE Champion; United States Champion; World Tag Team Champion; WWE Tag Team Champion; *Royal Rumble* Winner (2008)

STATS

 INTENSITY — 8

STRENGTH — 8

SPEED — 7

 COURAGE — 9

 BRAINS — 7

THE SHOWDOWN

Cena knows he has to act fast and furious when the match with Undertaker begins. He charges "the dead man," slamming into him with a mighty clothesline. But Undertaker doesn't move. He just glares at Cena and strikes back with a heavy hand, sending Cena to the mat. Cena digs deep and pulls himself back up to attack again.

Undertaker

YEARS ACTIVE: 1990–PRESENT

ATTRIBUTES

SIZE
AGILITY
STRENGTH

For well over two decades, the Undertaker his been an ominous force in the WWE. His power and in-ring skills seem almost supernatural, and his many championships prove it.

LEGEND'S ADVANTAGE
UNBEATABLE
Undefeated at *WrestleMania*

STATS

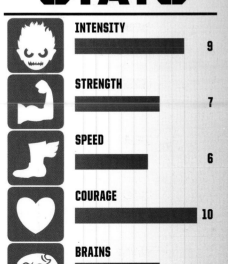

INTENSITY	9
STRENGTH	7
SPEED	6
COURAGE	10
BRAINS	7

INFO

6'10"	Height
299 lbs.	Weight
Death Valley	From
Chokeslam; Tombstone; Last Ride	Signature Move
WWE Champion; World Heavyweight Champion; World Tag Team Champion; WCW Tag Team Champion; Hardcore Champion; *WrestleMania* Undefeated Streak (20–0)	Career Highlights

The Miz and Diesel are both known for being smart—and for having big mouths. Those mouths have gotten them in trouble on more than one occasion, but they are usually able to use their incredible brains to escape. This time, though, after The Miz insulted Diesel, he wasn't able to think or talk a way out, leading to an explosive confrontation.

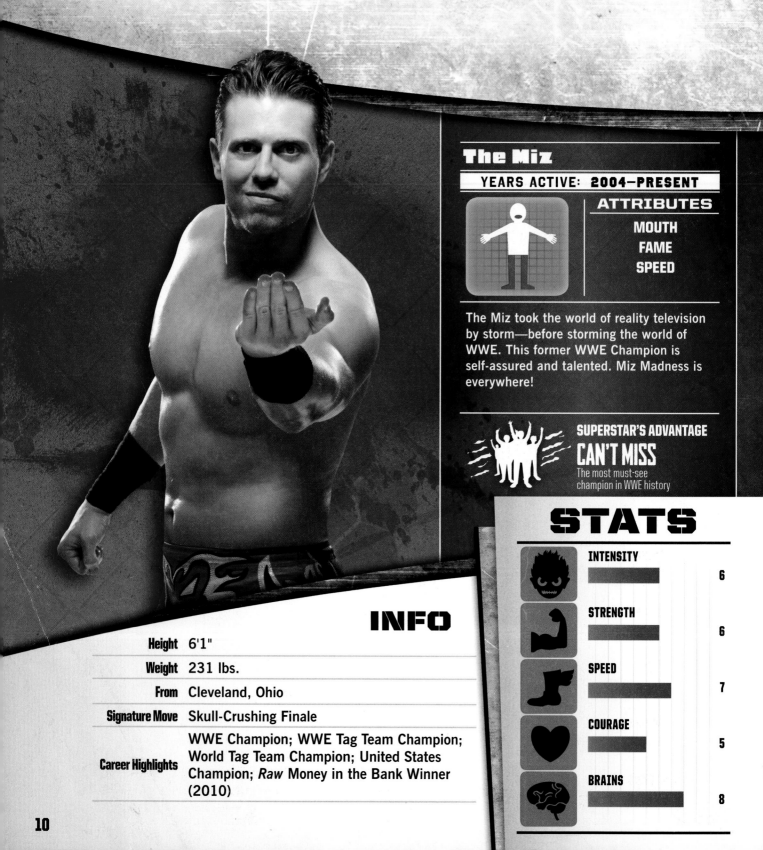

The Miz

YEARS ACTIVE: 2004–PRESENT

ATTRIBUTES

MOUTH
FAME
SPEED

The Miz took the world of reality television by storm—before storming the world of WWE. This former WWE Champion is self-assured and talented. Miz Madness is everywhere!

SUPERSTAR'S ADVANTAGE
CAN'T MISS
The most must-see champion in WWE history

STATS

	INTENSITY	6
	STRENGTH	6
	SPEED	7
	COURAGE	5
	BRAINS	8

INFO

Height	6'1"
Weight	231 lbs.
From	Cleveland, Ohio
Signature Move	Skull-Crushing Finale
Career Highlights	WWE Champion; WWE Tag Team Champion; World Tag Team Champion; United States Champion; *Raw* Money in the Bank Winner (2010)

THE SHOWDOWN

Standing a full 9 inches shorter than Diesel and being outweighed by nearly 100 pounds, The Miz faces a seemingly impossible challenge. Nevertheless, he decides to go on the offensive and aims full speed ahead at Diesel. "Big Daddy Cool" simply raises his foot. The Miz slams into Diesel's boot with his face.

Diesel (Kevin Nash)

YEARS ACTIVE: 1990–2004

ATTRIBUTES

SIZE
EXPERIENCE
SMARTS

Diesel—also known as Kevin Nash—was the longest-reigning WWE Champion of the '90s. Not only is he strong and capable but he's also intelligent, and those smarts pay off big time in the ring.

LEGEND'S ADVANTAGE
BRAINS
A brilliant strategist

STATS

INTENSITY		8
STRENGTH		8
SPEED		6
COURAGE		8
BRAINS		9

INFO

6'10"	Height
328 lbs.	Weight
Detroit, Michigan	From
Jackknife Powerbomb	Signature Move
WWE Champion; World Tag Team Champion; Intercontinental Champion; WCW World Heavyweight Champion; WCW Tag Team Champion	Career Highlights

11

Alberto Del Rio and JBL are extremely rich. The difference is Alberto inherited his wealth and life of privilege while JBL got his money the old-fashioned way: hard work. While both men flaunt their money and power, JBL is extremely annoyed by Alberto's arrogance about wealth he didn't earn. He wants nothing more than to teach the spoiled rich kid a lesson.

Alberto Del Rio

YEARS ACTIVE: 2010–PRESENT

ATTRIBUTES

WEALTH
POWER
PRIVILEGE

Royalty in Mexico, Alberto Del Rio has never wanted for anything, except the WWE Championship. He was taught the ways of the ring by his family in Mexico and brings an impressive background to WWE.

SUPERSTAR'S ADVANTAGE

HERITAGE
The son of Mexican royalty

STATS

INTENSITY		4
STRENGTH		6
SPEED		7
COURAGE		4
BRAINS		8

INFO

Height	6'5"
Weight	263 lbs.
From	San Luis Potosi, Mexico
Signature Move	Cross Armbreaker
Career Highlights	WWE Champion; World Heavyweight Champion; *Royal Rumble* Winner (2011); *Raw* Money in the Bank Winner (2011)

THE SHOWDOWN

Both Alberto and JBL drive their expensive cars to the ring. As JBL walks past Alberto's car, he pulls a crowbar from his belt and smashes one of the windows. This sends Alberto into a fury. He and JBL pummel each other, eventually making their way into the ring. JBL uses his size to push Alberto to the mat. Could Alberto be doomed?

JBL

YEARS ACTIVE: 1990–2009

ATTRIBUTES

TOUGHNESS
MEAN SPIRIT
SIZE

JBL likes money, but even more he likes to fight. He is a rough and tough cowboy at heart, even though he's rich. Don't make him angry, or you might find yourself on the receiving end of a vicious clothesline.

LEGEND'S ADVANTAGE
RUTHLESSNESS
Doesn't hold anything back

STATS

INTENSITY	7
STRENGTH	7
SPEED	6
COURAGE	7
BRAINS	8

INFO

6'6"	Height
290 lbs.	Weight
New York City, New York	From
Clothesline from Hell	Signature Move
WWE Champion; Intercontinental Champion; World Tag Team Champion; United States Champion; Hardcore Champion; European Champion	Career Highlights

When it comes to strong, tough fighters, they don't come stronger or tougher than Brock Lesnar and Batista. The two former champions are both expert professional wrestlers and mixed martial arts (MMA)-style competitors. Fighting is their favorite activity. Both are cold, mean warriors, determined to prove they are the best—but there can be only one best.

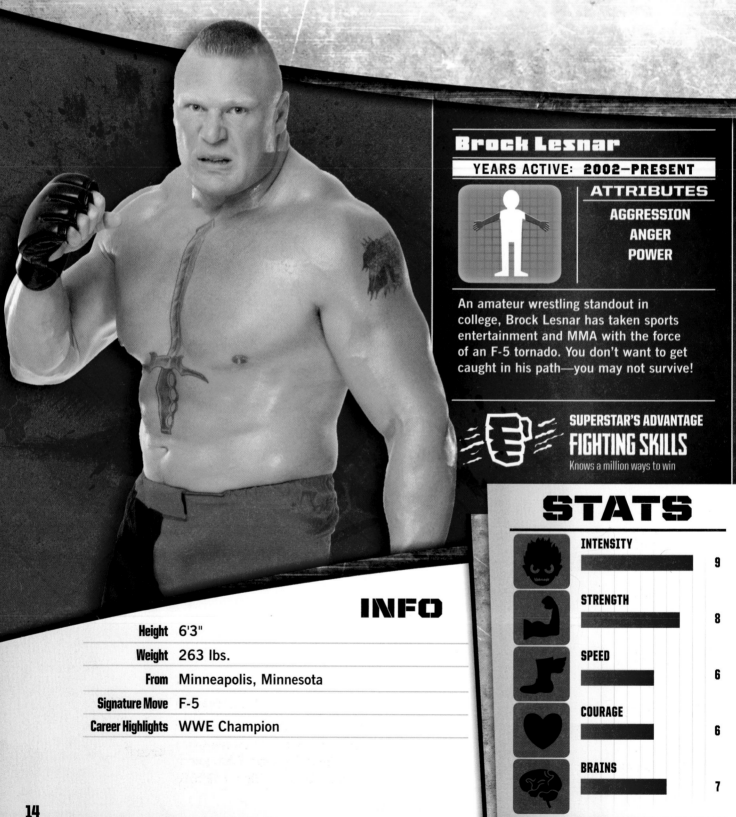

Brock Lesnar

YEARS ACTIVE: 2002–PRESENT

ATTRIBUTES

AGGRESSION
ANGER
POWER

An amateur wrestling standout in college, Brock Lesnar has taken sports entertainment and MMA with the force of an F-5 tornado. You don't want to get caught in his path—you may not survive!

SUPERSTAR'S ADVANTAGE

FIGHTING SKILLS

Knows a million ways to win

INFO

Height	6'3"
Weight	263 lbs.
From	Minneapolis, Minnesota
Signature Move	F-5
Career Highlights	WWE Champion

STATS

INTENSITY		9
STRENGTH		8
SPEED		6
COURAGE		6
BRAINS		7

THE SHOWDOWN

Sometimes WWE matches are displays of technical skill. Sometimes they feature beautiful aerial moves. Not this match! This is a good old-fashioned brawl. Lesnar and Batista attack each other with brutal hits and kicks. Each inflicts a lot of pain on his opponent, but neither man is willing to give up.

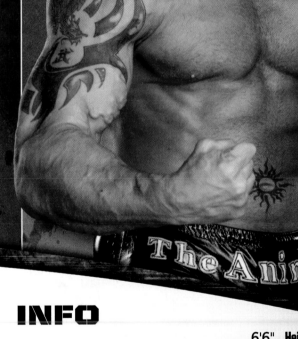

Batista

YEARS ACTIVE: 2002–2010

ATTRIBUTES

STRENGTH
POWER
INTENSITY

Tutored in sports entertainment by some of the best in the business, like Ric Flair and Triple H, Batista has shown he is a force to be reckoned with—but reckoning with him is not wise because he destroys opponents.

LEGEND'S ADVANTAGE
TRAINING
Taught by the best

STATS

INTENSITY	7
STRENGTH	9
SPEED	6
COURAGE	7
BRAINS	8

INFO

6'6"	Height
290 lbs.	Weight
Washington, DC	From
Batista Bomb	Signature Move
WWE Champion; World Heavyweight Champion; WWE Tag Team Champion; World Tag Team Champion; *Royal Rumble* Winner (2005)	Career Highlights

World Heavyweight Championship

In 1905, a professional wrestler named George Hackenschmidt was crowned the first World Heavyweight Wrestling Champion. George traveled around the country defending the championship in local wrestling events that were part of an organization called the National Wrestling Alliance (NWA). For nearly a hundred years, the World Heavyweight Champion competed in the NWA events until 2001, when the title was brought to the WWE. Since then, only WWE Superstars have competed for the title. Several legendary names like Dusty Rhodes, Harley Race, Edge, and Sheamus have been heavyweight champs.

Sheamus and The Rock are two of the most colorful personalities in WWE. Though they have never had an issue, with the World Heavyweight Championship on the line, a match between these fierce competitors would be extremely intense. With fan favorites equally determined to win the title, choosing a side will prove difficult for the WWE Universe.

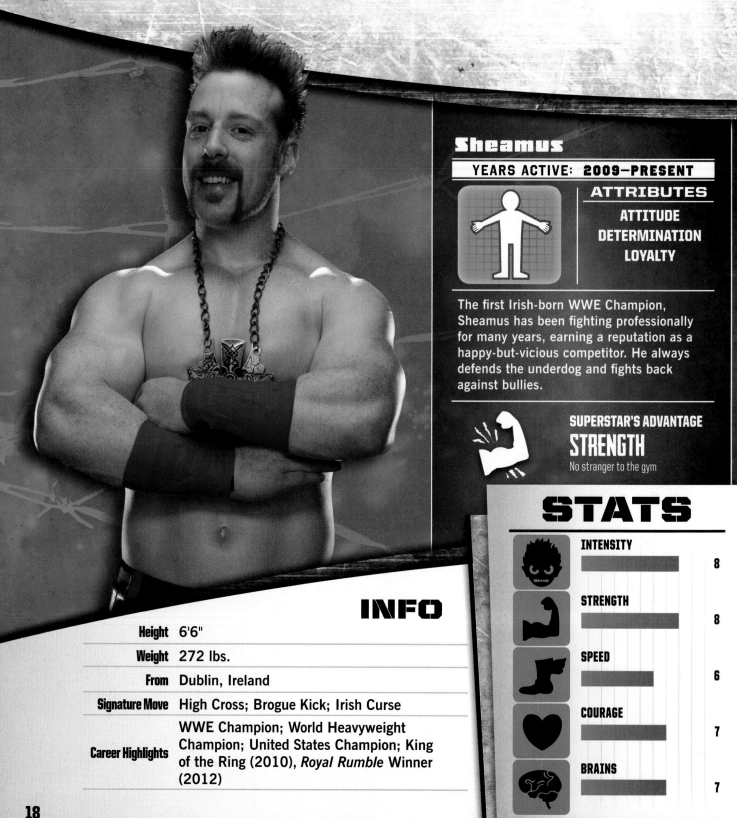

Sheamus

YEARS ACTIVE: 2009–PRESENT

ATTRIBUTES

ATTITUDE
DETERMINATION
LOYALTY

The first Irish-born WWE Champion, Sheamus has been fighting professionally for many years, earning a reputation as a happy-but-vicious competitor. He always defends the underdog and fights back against bullies.

SUPERSTAR'S ADVANTAGE
STRENGTH
No stranger to the gym

INFO

Height	6'6"
Weight	272 lbs.
From	Dublin, Ireland
Signature Move	High Cross; Brogue Kick; Irish Curse
Career Highlights	WWE Champion; World Heavyweight Champion; United States Champion; King of the Ring (2010), *Royal Rumble* Winner (2012)

STATS

INTENSITY		8
STRENGTH		8
SPEED		6
COURAGE		7
BRAINS		7

THE SHOWDOWN

The match begins with a friendly, almost joking shove. Then a light slap. And suddenly Sheamus and The Rock both leap into action and the friendliness is dropped. Sheamus levels The Rock with a clothesline, but The Rock springs off his back onto his feet. Sheamus tries a big kick, but misses. The Rock only laughs as he kicks back.

The Rock

YEARS ACTIVE: 1996–PRESENT

ATTRIBUTES
PERSONALITY
HERITAGE
TALENT

Known as "the most electrifying man in all of entertainment," The Rock has made his name known in WWE, in Hollywood, and around the world. A third-generation Superstar (both his father and grandfather were also wrestlers), The Rock will forever be "the people's champion."

LEGEND'S ADVANTAGE
MAN OF THE PEOPLE
Electrifies the audience

STATS

INTENSITY		7
STRENGTH		8
SPEED		8
COURAGE		8
BRAINS		9

INFO

6'5"	Height
260 lbs.	Weight
Miami, Florida	From
Rock Bottom; People's Elbow	Signature Move
WWE Champion; Intercontinental Champion; World Tag Team Champion; *Royal Rumble* Winner (2000); WCW Champion	Career Highlights

BIG SHOW vs. YOKOZUNA

If you combine the weight of these two competitors, it totals more than half a ton. Both Big Show and Yokozuna are among the greatest super heavyweights in history. They are also both former champions and claim to be among the largest athletes in the world. A one-on-one matchup between these two icons would go a long way to determine who is the best "big man" in the history of WWE.

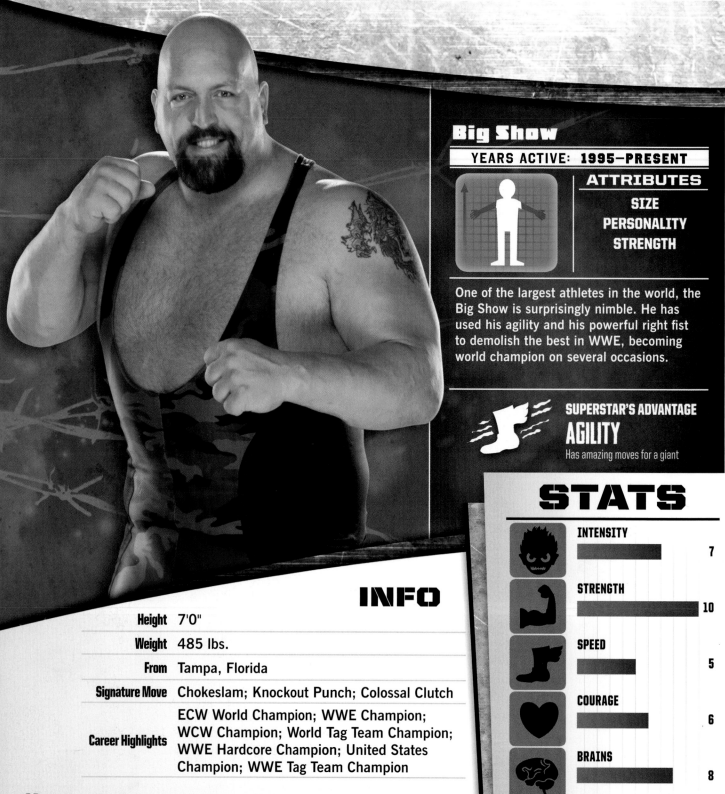

Big Show

YEARS ACTIVE: 1995–PRESENT

ATTRIBUTES

SIZE
PERSONALITY
STRENGTH

One of the largest athletes in the world, the Big Show is surprisingly nimble. He has used his agility and his powerful right fist to demolish the best in WWE, becoming world champion on several occasions.

SUPERSTAR'S ADVANTAGE
AGILITY
Has amazing moves for a giant

INFO

Height	7'0"
Weight	485 lbs.
From	Tampa, Florida
Signature Move	Chokeslam; Knockout Punch; Colossal Clutch
Career Highlights	ECW World Champion; WWE Champion; WCW Champion; World Tag Team Champion; WWE Hardcore Champion; United States Champion; WWE Tag Team Champion

STATS

INTENSITY		7
STRENGTH		10
SPEED		5
COURAGE		6
BRAINS		8

THE SHOWDOWN

Because of the sheer size of these two competitors, WWE officials first have to make sure that the ring is reinforced to support their weight. When the bell rings, these two giants move slowly toward each other and lock up, each trying to shove the other backward to no avail. Finally, mustering all of his strength, Big Show forces Yokozuna down to the mat, causing the entire arena floor to shake.

Yokozuna

YEARS ACTIVE: 1992–1998

ATTRIBUTES

SIZE
POWER
LEGACY

With his manager Mr. Fuji always in his corner, Yokozuna uses his giant size to squash countless opponents. His dreaded Banzai Drop—where he jumps off the middle rope, landing on his opponents—has won him several titles.

LEGEND'S ADVANTAGE

EXPERIENCE

An accomplished sumo wrestler and Superstar

STATS

INTENSITY		6
STRENGTH		8
SPEED		4
COURAGE		5
BRAINS		6

INFO

6'4"	Height
589 lbs.	Weight
The Land of the Rising Sun	From
Banzai Drop	Signature Move
WWE Champion; World Tag Team Champion; *Royal Rumble* Winner (1993)	Career Highlights

Daniel Bryan and Booker T are two proud men who hate to lose. Bryan is a technical wizard in the ring while Booker T is more of a brawler. But they both brought a certain level of prestige to the World Heavyweight Championship. Daniel Bryan hasn't always gotten along with fans, but Booker T always tries to entertain and support the fans.

Daniel Bryan

YEARS ACTIVE: 2009–PRESENT

ATTRIBUTES

SPEED
TALENT
WISDOM

After making his name in independent wrestling promotions all over the world, Daniel Bryan arrived in WWE and immediately made an impact as part of the Nexus. Now he's on his own, angry, and hungry to show the world he's the best.

SUPERSTAR'S ADVANTAGE
WORLDLY WISE
Competed worldwide

INFO

Height	5'10"
Weight	192 lbs.
From	Aberdeen, Washington
Signature Move	"No" Lock
Career Highlights	World Heavyweight Champion; United States Champion; *SmackDown!* Money in the Bank Winner (2011); trained by Shawn Michaels and William Regal

STATS

INTENSITY	5
STRENGTH	7
SPEED	7
COURAGE	7
BRAINS	7

THE SHOWDOWN

As Booker and Bryan meet in the center of the ring, Bryan extends his hand in a show of sportsmanship. Booker shakes Bryan's hand, but is surprised when Bryan strikes him in the face with his other hand. Booker snaps, returning the blow and then hitting Bryan with a quick dropkick. The kick sends Bryan falling backward, smacking into the referee as he falls.

Booker T

YEARS ACTIVE: 1993–2007

ATTRIBUTES
EXPERIENCE
LEADERSHIP
BRAVERY

Booker T competed with his brother in the popular tag team Harlem Heat before breaking out on his own. He won the World Heavyweight Championship five times in WCW, and then conquered WWE by winning the title again.

LEGEND'S ADVANTAGE
KNOWLEDGE
Knows the business from every angle

STATS

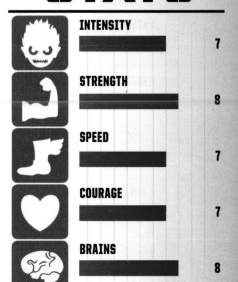

INTENSITY	7
STRENGTH	8
SPEED	7
COURAGE	7
BRAINS	8

INFO

6'3"	Height
253 lbs.	Weight
Houston, Texas	From
Axe Kick, Spinarooni	Signature Move
World Heavyweight Champion; WCW Champion; World Tag Team Champion; WCW Tag Team Champion; Intercontinental Champion; United States Champion; WCW Television Champion; Hardcore Champion; King of the Ring (2006)	Career Highlights

Randy Orton and Diamond Dallas Page use the same signature move. Orton calls it the RKO while DDP—who invented the move—calls it the Diamond Cutter. Page wants to teach Orton a lesson in respecting one's elders, but Orton has never had respect for the so-called Legends in WWE. In fact, he used to call himself the Legend Killer. Orton is ready to teach DDP how dangerous he is.

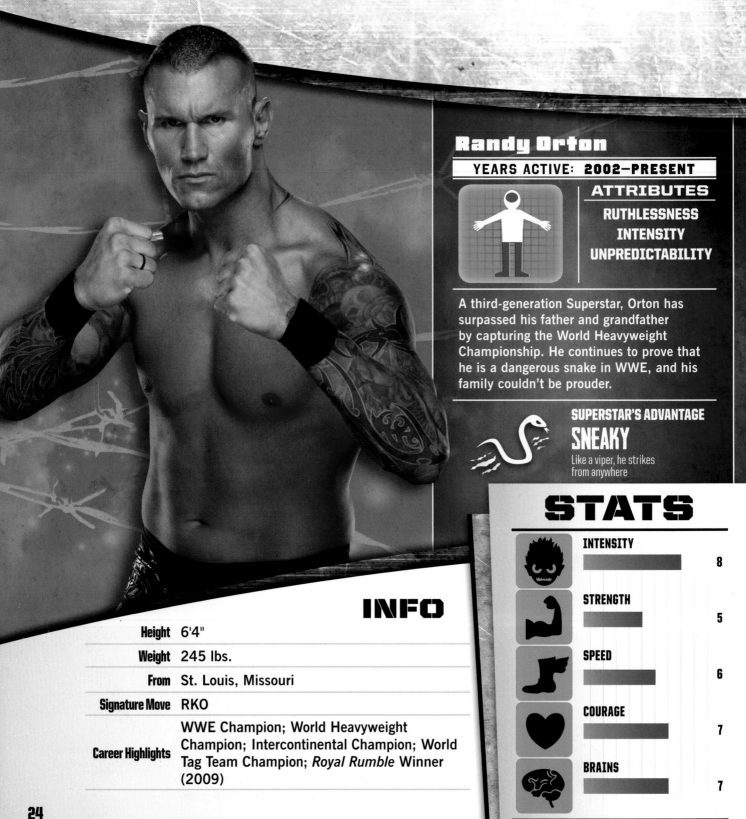

Randy Orton

YEARS ACTIVE: 2002–PRESENT

ATTRIBUTES

RUTHLESSNESS

INTENSITY

UNPREDICTABILITY

A third-generation Superstar, Orton has surpassed his father and grandfather by capturing the World Heavyweight Championship. He continues to prove that he is a dangerous snake in WWE, and his family couldn't be prouder.

SUPERSTAR'S ADVANTAGE

SNEAKY

Like a viper, he strikes from anywhere

STATS

INTENSITY	8
STRENGTH	5
SPEED	6
COURAGE	7
BRAINS	7

INFO

Height	6'4"
Weight	245 lbs.
From	St. Louis, Missouri
Signature Move	RKO
Career Highlights	WWE Champion; World Heavyweight Champion; Intercontinental Champion; World Tag Team Champion; *Royal Rumble* Winner (2009)

THE SHOWDOWN

Orton and DDP circle each other in the ring, each glaring and daring the other to make the first move. It's the "Viper" Orton who springs the first attack. He leaps at DDP, driving an elbow into his face. The Legend quickly shakes it off and fires back with a series of elbows of his own.

Diamond Dallas Page

YEARS ACTIVE: 1995–2002

ATTRIBUTES
POPULARITY
WISDOM
AGILITY

DDP began his sports entertainment career as a manager, but learned the business so well that he transitioned to being a competitor in the ring. He became a World Champion multiple times.

LEGEND'S ADVANTAGE
FLEXIBILITY
From being a yoga master

STATS

INTENSITY		7
STRENGTH		5
SPEED		8
COURAGE		7
BRAINS		7

INFO

6'5"	Height
248 lbs.	Weight
The Jersey Shore	From
Diamond Cutter	Signature Move
WCW World Heavyweight Champion; United States Champion; European Champion; WCW World Television Champion; WCW World Tag Team Champion; World Tag Team Champion	Career Highlights

It's the "Real American" Jack Swagger against "The American Dream" Dusty Rhodes. Despite their similar nicknames, these two competitors couldn't be more different. Rhodes is a champion for the common man. He believes in hard work and the simple life. Swagger is talented—so his success has come naturally. And he loves the attention his arrogance gets him.

Jack Swagger

YEARS ACTIVE: 2008–PRESENT

ATTRIBUTES

TALENT
MOUTH
SNEAKINESS

Jack Swagger was one of the best amateur wrestlers in the world prior to entering WWE. Upon his arrival, he bragged about his talent—and backed it up by winning matches and championships.

SUPERSTAR'S ADVANTAGE

CHAMPIONSHIPS

A master both in amateur ranks and WWE

INFO

Height	6'6"
Weight	263 lbs.
From	Perry, Oklahoma
Signature Move	Ankle Lock; Gutwrench Power Bomb
Career Highlights	World Heavyweight Champion; ECW Champion; *Raw* Money in the Bank Winner (2010)

STATS

	INTENSITY	8
	STRENGTH	7
	SPEED	8
	COURAGE	6
	BRAINS	6

THE SHOWDOWN

Jack Swagger uses his superior speed and agility to hit and run on Rhodes. Rhodes tries to grab Swagger in a bear hug, but Swagger dodges. Swagger mockingly imitates Dusty Rhodes's famous dance moves in the center of the ring. Insulted, The American Dream runs at Swagger, but he dodges again. Frustrated, Rhodes moves to the corner, coming up with a plan of attack.

Dusty Rhodes

YEARS ACTIVE: 1968–1991

ATTRIBUTES
POPULARITY
FEARLESSNESS
DANCE MOVES

A hero to the "common man," Dusty Rhodes chose his nickname, "The American Dream," because he wants everyone to understand the power that dream has—anyone can grow up to be successful and happy—and win championships.

LEGEND'S ADVANTAGE
WISDOM
One of the best teachers in all of WWE

STATS

INTENSITY		6
STRENGTH		6
SPEED		7
COURAGE		10
BRAINS		7

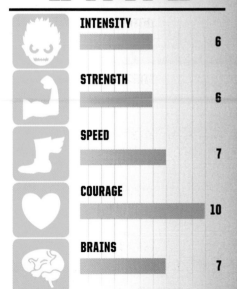

INFO

6'2"	Height
300 lbs.	Weight
Austin, Texas	From
Bionic Elbow	Signature Move
NWA World Champion; NWA World Tag Team Champion; United States Champion; NWA Television Champion; 1987 Crockett Cup Tag Team Tournament Winner (with Nikita Koloff)	Career Highlights

27

Intercontinental Championship

While the WWE Championship is universally accepted as the biggest prize in sports entertainment, the Intercontinental Championship is known for its link to countless Superstars and Legends with superior technical skills. Often, winning the Intercontinental Championship has catapulted WWE Superstars into big main events—and sometimes on to winning the WWE Championship. Ever since the Intercontinental Championship was first won by WWE Hall of Famer Pat Patterson in 1979, many big names have held it, including Ricky Steamboat, Razor Ramon, The Miz, and Kofi Kingston.

When new Superstars begin their WWE careers, they are often told to watch videos of Ricky Steamboat matches to find out the best way to perform in the ring. Kofi Kingston has the rare privilege of getting in the ring with the best of all time and learning from him. Steamboat loves teaching, and Kofi is ready to learn.

Kofi Kingston

YEARS ACTIVE: 2007–PRESENT

ATTRIBUTES

SPEED
AGILITY
ATTITUDE

A high-flying, life-loving Superstar, Kofi Kingston is superfast and has an arsenal of moves that let him soar from the top rope through the air, taking opponents by surprise.

SUPERSTAR'S ADVANTAGE
ENTHUSIASM
Full of youthful excitement

INFO

Height	6'1"
Weight	221 lbs.
From	Ghana, West Africa
Signature Move	Trouble in Paradise
Career Highlights	Intercontinental Champion; World Tag Team Champion; United States Champion

STATS

INTENSITY		5
STRENGTH		6
SPEED		9
COURAGE		7
BRAINS		8

THE SHOWDOWN

Kofi and Steamboat begin their match tying up in each other's arms. Steamboat pulls Kofi in and flips him to the ground with an arm drag. Kofi springs to his feet and strikes back on Steamboat with a big surprise kick. Steamboat isn't on the mat for long, though. He leaps back to his feet and unleashes a series of kicks on Kofi's torso.

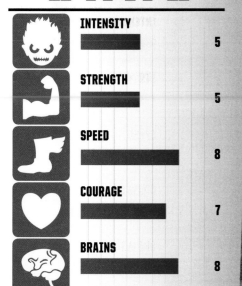

Ricky Steamboat

YEARS ACTIVE: 1976–1994

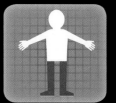

ATTRIBUTES

SPEED

AGILITY

TRAINING

Throughout his career, Ricky "The Dragon" Steamboat was known for stealing the show whenever he competed. His matches were a thing of technical beauty, inspiring generations of WWE Superstars to be the best they can be.

LEGEND'S ADVANTAGE
TECHNICAL SKILL
Best arm drag in WWE history

STATS

INTENSITY		5
STRENGTH		5
SPEED		8
COURAGE		7
BRAINS		8

INFO

5'10"	Height
235 lbs.	Weight
Honolulu, Hawaii	From
Arm Drag	Signature Move
NWA World Heavyweight Champion; WWE Intercontinental Champion; WCW United States Champion; WCW World Tag Team Champion	Career Highlights

DOLPH ZIGGLER vs. MR. PERFECT

They say nobody's perfect, but Dolph Ziggler and Mr. Perfect disagree. Both men claim to be the embodiment of perfection. With great arrogance, each boasts of being the best in sports entertainment and in all other aspects of life. Proving that you're perfect means never losing—even to someone else who says they're perfect.

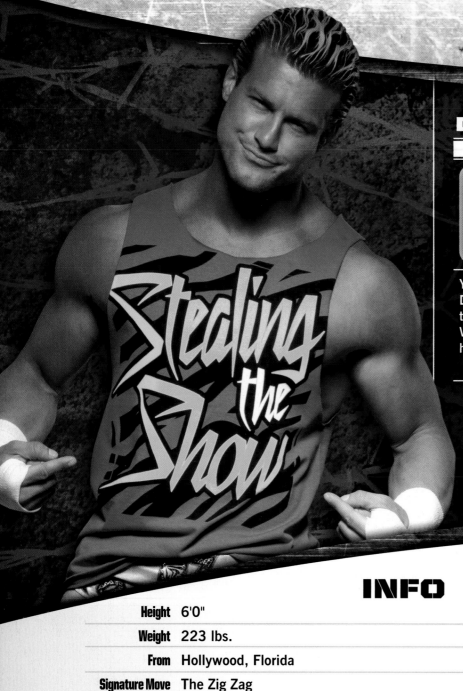

Dolph Ziggler

YEARS ACTIVE: 2005—PRESENT

ATTRIBUTES

LOOKS
SPEED
TALENT

Young, brash, and extremely talented, Dolph Ziggler knows without any doubt that he is the best Superstar in all of the WWE. His motto is "I am perfection," and he lives up to it every night in the ring.

 SUPERSTAR'S ADVANTAGE
SPEED
Don't blink or you'll miss him

INFO

Height	6'0"
Weight	223 lbs.
From	Hollywood, Florida
Signature Move	The Zig Zag
Career Highlights	World Heavyweight Champion; Intercontinental Champion

STATS

 INTENSITY — 6

 STRENGTH — 6

 SPEED — 9

 COURAGE — 5

BRAINS — 4

THE SHOWDOWN

In the blink of an eye, Ziggler and Perfect put holds and counterholds on each other. Ziggler smothers Perfect in a half nelson, but Perfect slips out and ties Ziggler up in an abdominal stretch. Ziggler counters, reversing the abdominal stretch on Perfect. Perfect slips out of the hold and pulls Ziggler to the mat by his ankles.

Mr. Perfect

YEARS ACTIVE: 1980–2002

ATTRIBUTES
TALENT
SMARTS
QUICKNESS

Mr. Perfect wins at everything he tries: wrestling, baseball, football, swimming, chess, darts, and more! In the ring, he is flawless, showing off his supreme skills and wrestling savvy.

LEGEND'S ADVANTAGE
PERFECTION
Absolutely perfect at everything he does

STATS

INTENSITY	5
STRENGTH	6
SPEED	9
COURAGE	5
BRAINS	8

INFO

6'3"	Height
235 lbs.	Weight
Robbinsdale, Minnesota	From
Perfect-Plex	Signature Move
AWA World Champion; Intercontinental Champion; United States Champion; WCW Tag Team Champion; AWA World Tag Team Champion	Career Highlights

Merry ol' England is known for a lot of things: the Royal Family, Big Ben, fish and chips—and some of the best warriors to ever battle in a wrestling ring, including William Regal and "The British Bulldog" Davey Boy Smith. These two Brit Superstars love their native country, and love punishing opponents in the ring even more. Though their home country is the same, their styles couldn't be more different: Regal is a brawler, while the Bulldog is a powerhouse.

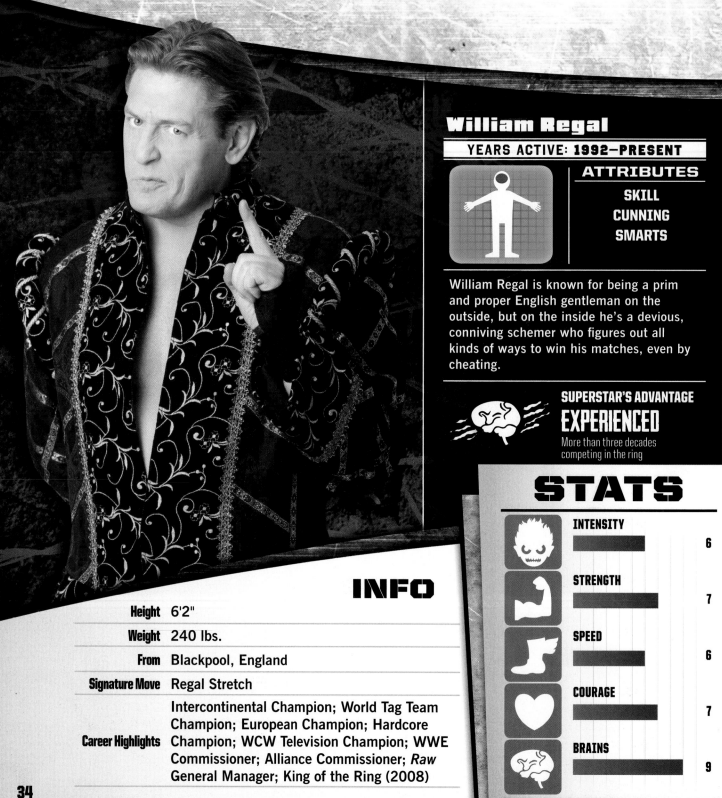

William Regal

YEARS ACTIVE: 1992–PRESENT

ATTRIBUTES

SKILL
CUNNING
SMARTS

William Regal is known for being a prim and proper English gentleman on the outside, but on the inside he's a devious, conniving schemer who figures out all kinds of ways to win his matches, even by cheating.

SUPERSTAR'S ADVANTAGE

EXPERIENCED

More than three decades competing in the ring

INFO

Height	6'2"
Weight	240 lbs.
From	Blackpool, England
Signature Move	Regal Stretch
Career Highlights	Intercontinental Champion; World Tag Team Champion; European Champion; Hardcore Champion; WCW Television Champion; WWE Commissioner; Alliance Commissioner; *Raw* General Manager; King of the Ring (2008)

STATS

INTENSITY		6
STRENGTH		7
SPEED		6
COURAGE		7
BRAINS		9

THE SHOWDOWN

Regal wants to start a fistfight with the Bulldog, but Davey Boy doesn't give him the chance. He hoists his fellow countryman up high into the air and drops him to the mat with a hard-thudding body slam. Regal gets back up, but it's not quick. His back hurts from hitting the mat so hard. The Bulldog scoops him up and body slams him down again.

The British Bulldog

YEARS ACTIVE: 1984-2000

ATTRIBUTES
STRENGTH
HERITAGE
HAPPINESS

Superstrong competitor "The British Bulldog" Davey Boy Smith was feared by his opponents and loved by his allies. He was a member of the legendary Hart Foundation.

LEGEND'S ADVANTAGE
POWER
One of the strongest men ever in WWE

STATS

Stat	Value
INTENSITY	6
STRENGTH	9
SPEED	8
COURAGE	7
BRAINS	7

INFO

5'11"	Height
260 lbs.	Weight
Manchester, England	From
Running Powerslam	Signature Move
World Tag Team Champion; European Champion; Intercontinental Champion; Hardcore Champion	Career Highlights

CODY RHODES vs. RAVISHING RICK RUDE

Dashing and *Ravishing* aren't usually words that people associate with the Superstars and Legends of the WWE, but with Cody Rhodes and Rick Rude, they are completely appropriate. Both men take great pride in their physical appearance. When a man is so concerned with his appearance, he doesn't want anyone to look better than him—and will fight anyone who challenges his good looks.

Cody Rhodes

YEARS ACTIVE: 2007–PRESENT

ATTRIBUTES

LOOKS

HERITAGE

SPEED

The son of WWE Hall of Famer "The American Dream" Dusty Rhodes, Cody has genetic gifts that make him a standout in the ring and "Dashing" outside the ring.

 SUPERSTAR'S ADVANTAGE

GENETICS

Dusty Rhodes is his dad

INFO

Height	6'1"
Weight	223 lbs.
From	Marietta, Georgia
Signature Move	Cross Rhodes
Career Highlights	World Tag Team Champion; WWE Tag Team Champion; son of WWE Hall of Famer "The American Dream" Dusty Rhodes

STATS

INTENSITY		6
STRENGTH		6
SPEED		8
COURAGE		5
BRAINS		7

THE SHOWDOWN

Ravishing Rick enters the ring and poses for the audience, allowing Rhodes to sneak in and hit him from behind. Rude retaliates with several hard hits that send Rhodes to the corner, covering his beautiful face. Rude steps back to again pose for the audience, and again Rhodes hits Rude with an atomic drop from behind, causing Rude to favor his now-sore tailbone.

Ravishing Rick Rude

YEARS ACTIVE: 1984–1994

ATTRIBUTES

STRENGTH
SPEED
BRAINS

Ravishing Rick Rude had an amazing physique, and made sure you knew it. He would wear elaborate robes to the ring and pose, flexing his impressive muscles for the WWE Universe.

LEGEND'S ADVANTAGE

MANAGERS

Always has someone watching his back competing in the ring

STATS

INTENSITY		6
STRENGTH		8
SPEED		8
COURAGE		6
BRAINS		8

INFO

6'3"	Height
252 lbs.	Weight
Robbinsdale, Minnesota	From
Rude Awakening	Signature Move
Intercontinental Champion; WCW International World Heavyweight Champion	Career Highlights

United States Championship

The National Wrestling Alliance, a group of small-time wrestling promotions that began in the early 1900s, had the World Heavyweight Champion, who traveled around the country competing in different territories. The number one contender to the NWA World Heavyweight Championship was always the United States Champion. The United States Championship might have been considered by some to be the second best title in the NWA, but don't tell that to Legends like Steve Austin, Booker T, Dusty Rhodes, Diamond Dallas Page, and the many others who won it. In 2001, it was brought to WWE, where it's been exclusively competed for ever since.

ANTONIO CESARO vs. "ROWDY" RODDY PIPER

They say opposites attract, and maybe that's true if the opposites are attracted to fight each other. Antonio Cesaro and "Rowdy" Roddy Piper couldn't be more unlike each other if they tried. Cesaro is disciplined, focused, and aggressive, while Piper is a swing-first-ask-questions-later type of wild man. Cesaro has the precision of an army knife from his native Switzerland, while Piper hits anywhere, anytime without thinking.

Antonio Cesaro

YEARS ACTIVE: 2012–PRESENT

ATTRIBUTES
UNSTOPPABILITY
INTENSITY
AGGRESSIVENESS

Antonio Cesaro speaks five languages, is an accomplished professional rugby player, and a retired military man. His focus and intensity are matched only by his raw talent—which is amazing.

 SUPERSTAR'S ADVANTAGE
PRIDE
He's a proud Swiss warrior

INFO

Height	6'5"
Weight	232 lbs.
From	Lucerne, Switzerland
Signature Move	The Neutralizer
Career Highlights	United States Champion

STATS

INTENSITY	9
STRENGTH	7
SPEED	7
COURAGE	7
BRAINS	9

THE SHOWDOWN

Cesaro enters the ring, thinking that his finely honed skills will be no match for the Rowdy One. He's surprised when Piper comes at him like a cartoon Tasmanian devil, swinging and kicking without rhyme or reason. Cesaro tries to rework his strategy, but Piper is going entirely on instinct. Cesaro knows you can't reason with a wild animal, and that's just what Piper is acting like!

"Rowdy" Roddy Piper

YEARS ACTIVE: 1973–2000

ATTRIBUTES
SCRAP
MOUTH
DETERMINATION

Part of WWE since before the first *WrestleMania*, "Rowdy" Roddy Piper is unpredictable to say the least. After all, his motto is "Just when you think you've got the answers, I change the questions!"

LEGEND'S ADVANTAGE
WILDNESS
You think you know how he fights, then he changes it up

STATS

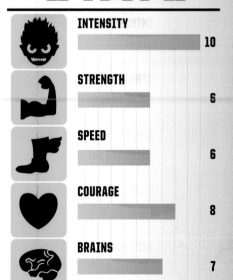

INTENSITY — 10

STRENGTH — 6

SPEED — 6

COURAGE — 8

BRAINS — 7

INFO

6'2"	Height
235 lbs.	Weight
Glasgow, Scotland	From
Sleeper Hold	Signature Move
Intercontinental Champion; United States Champion; World Tag Team Champion	Career Highlights

Zack Ryder is known as a funny, entertaining guy. Greg "The Hammer" Valentine is all business. Their battle in the ring is not only a clash of wrestling styles but of completely opposite personalities. They are so different that you might wonder how they ever got together in the ring. It's all about the pride of being the United States Champion, a title both men have held in their careers and will forever boast about.

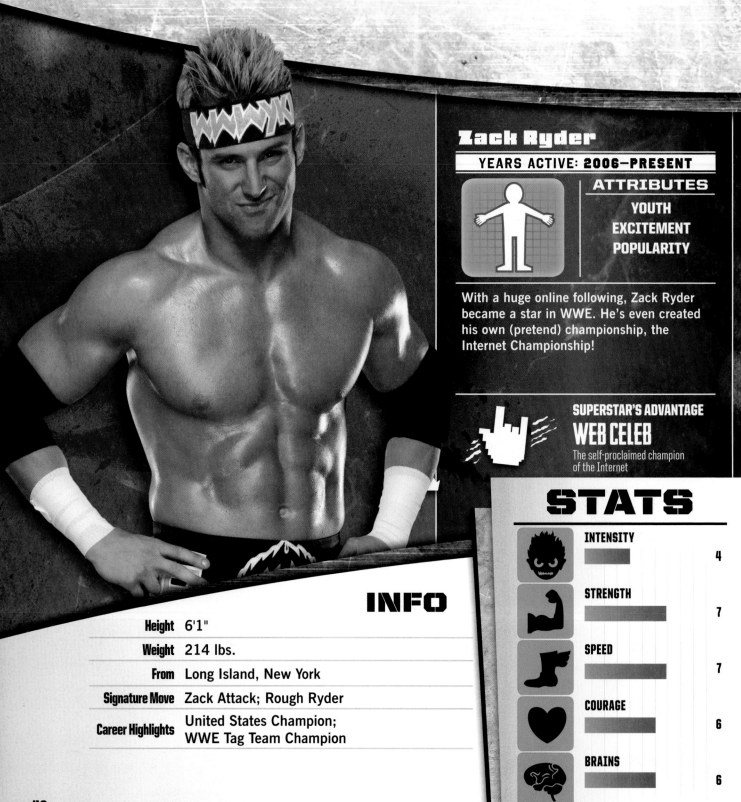

Zack Ryder

YEARS ACTIVE: 2006–PRESENT

ATTRIBUTES

YOUTH
EXCITEMENT
POPULARITY

With a huge online following, Zack Ryder became a star in WWE. He's even created his own (pretend) championship, the Internet Championship!

SUPERSTAR'S ADVANTAGE

WEB CELEB

The self-proclaimed champion of the Internet

STATS

INTENSITY		4
STRENGTH		7
SPEED		7
COURAGE		6
BRAINS		6

INFO

Height	6'1"
Weight	214 lbs.
From	Long Island, New York
Signature Move	Zack Attack; Rough Ryder
Career Highlights	United States Champion; WWE Tag Team Champion

THE SHOWDOWN

Before the match, Ryder uses his mobile phone to try to record an interview with Valentine for Ryder's Internet video show, *Z True Long Island Story*. Valentine gets mad and slaps the phone out of Ryder's hand. Ryder looks shocked and confused—but only for a second because Valentine then smacks Ryder's face!

Greg Valentine

YEARS ACTIVE: 1970–1994

ATTRIBUTES

TOUGHNESS
COMMITMENT
HARD HITS

Greg Valentine is so tough that he has the perfect nickname: The Hammer. A huge star in the 1970s and '80s, The Hammer taught thousands of opponents what it means to be hit hard.

LEGEND'S ADVANTAGE
TOUGH
Built like a steel hammer

STATS

INTENSITY	8
STRENGTH	7
SPEED	6
COURAGE	6
BRAINS	6

INFO

6'0"	Height
243 lbs.	Weight
Seattle, Washington	From
Figure-Four Leglock	Signature Move
United States Champion; Intercontinental Champion	Career Highlights

Neither Santino Marella nor "Hacksaw" Jim Duggan is really considered to be the most serious of WWE Superstars or Legends, but they are both loved by the WWE Universe because they are entertaining. Santino has done some wacky stuff in his career, like dressing as his "sister" for a Divas battle, while Duggan's battle cry of "Hooooooooo!" gets the crowd ready for action.

Santino Marella

YEARS ACTIVE: 2007–PRESENT

ATTRIBUTES

HUMOR
HAPPINESS
PERSEVERANCE

Santino Marella was picked out of the audience to compete for the Intercontinental Championship when WWE toured Italy. He won the title that night, and his life has not been the same since.

SUPERSTAR'S ADVANTAGE
SURPRISE
Never know when he'll strike

INFO

Height	5'10"
Weight	227 lbs.
From	Calabria, Italy
Signature Move	The Cobra
Career Highlights	Intercontinental Champion; WWE Tag Team Champion

STATS

INTENSITY		3
STRENGTH		5
SPEED		6
COURAGE		4
BRAINS		4

THE SHOWDOWN

Santino is the first to enter the ring. When Hacksaw arrives, he's got his trusty two-by-four in hand and swings it over his head. Santino ducks in the corner, protecting himself from Duggan's piece of lumber. Duggan marches around the ring, chanting "U-S-A! U-S-A!" with the crowd, waving the wooden plank in the air to mass applause as the opening bell rings.

"Hacksaw" Jim Duggan

YEARS ACTIVE: 1979–2009

ATTRIBUTES

GUTS
BRAVERY
POPULARITY

"Hacksaw" Jim Duggan loves the United States of America. A patriotic Legend, he has been known to bring Old Glory with him to the ring and salute the members of the Armed Forces everywhere he goes.

LEGEND'S ADVANTAGE

TEAM AMERICA

His nation always supports him

STATS

INTENSITY		5
STRENGTH		6
SPEED		6
COURAGE		7
BRAINS		5

INFO

6'3"	Height
270 lbs.	Weight
Glens Falls, New York	From
Three-Point Stance Clothesline	Signature Move
United States Champion; WCW Television Champion; first-ever *Royal Rumble* Winner (1988)	Career Highlights

Tag Team Championship

Having a partner to watch your back and help you compete in the ring is a big advantage—and the reason that tag teams were formed in the first place. In 1971, WWE introduced the Tag Team Championship, legitimizing the tag team style of in-ring competition. Since that time, WWE Superstars have found partners to team up with, and together they prove their dominance in the tag team division of sports entertainment. Many legendary Superstars first made their name in tag teams, such as Shawn Michaels (a member of The Rockers), Steve Austin (a member of the Hollywood Blondes), and Kevin Nash (as a member of the Dudes with Attitudes).

Arguably the greatest tag team of all time, the Road Warriors have little patience for anyone who wants to challenge them. But for Epico and Primo, who are part of Puerto Rico wrestling's legendary Colon family, defeating the Road Warriors is a must. They want to show the WWE Universe, the other Superstars and Legends, and even their own family, that they are better than the best.

Primo and Epico

YEARS ACTIVE: 2008–PRESENT

ATTRIBUTES

QUICKNESS
TALENT
FAMILY

Sports entertainment is in the blood of Primo and Epico. As the son (Primo) and nephew (Epico) of legendary wrestling promoter Carlos Colon, these Latin stars know how to win matches.

SUPERSTAR'S ADVANTAGE
HERITAGE
Taught by their legendary father/uncle

INFO

Height	6'2"/ 5'10"
Weight	217 lbs./ 215 lbs.
From	San Juan, Puerto Rico
Signature Move	Backstabber; Backbreaker
Career Highlights	WWE Tag Team Champions

STATS

INTENSITY		5
STRENGTH		5
SPEED		9
COURAGE		6
BRAINS		5

THE SHOWDOWN

The Road Warriors remove their fearsome spiked shoulder pads and stand side-by-side in the center of the ring staring down Primo and Epico. The two young, eager Superstars charge Hawk and Animal at full speed. They collide with the Legends, and it's as though they ran into brick walls. Neither Road Warrior moves, but Primo and Epico fall backward from the force of their collision.

The Road Warriors

YEARS ACTIVE: 1983–2003

ATTRIBUTES

STRENGTH

INTENSITY

POWER

From the mean streets of Chicago, Hawk and Animal are tough, powerful, and nasty. Their war paint and shoulder pads strike fear in the hearts of every opponent who faces them in the ring.

LEGEND'S ADVANTAGE

TOUGHNESS

The toughest tag team to ever compete in WWE

STATS

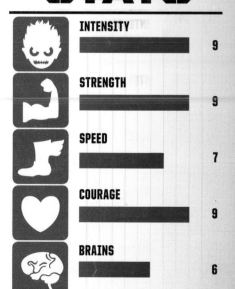

INTENSITY		9
STRENGTH		9
SPEED		7
COURAGE		9
BRAINS		6

INFO

6'2"/ 6'2"	**Height**
277 lbs./ 305 lbs.	**Weight**
Chicago, Illinois	**From**
Doomsday Device	**Signature Move**
World Tag Team Champions; AWA World Tag Team Champions; NWA National Tag Team Champions; NWA International Tag Team Champions	**Career Highlights**

THE USOS vs. THE WILD SAMOANS

The Isle of Samoa has produced numerous successful WWE Superstars, including The Rock and Yokozuna. Among the first of these legendary stars were the Wild Samoans, Afa and Sika. They competed all over the world and are a fearsome combination. Their nephews, the Uso twins, continue to represent their home island proudly in WWE and want to show their uncles that they are deserving heirs of the Samoan legacy.

The Usos

YEARS ACTIVE: 2010—PRESENT

ATTRIBUTES

SPEED
SMARTS
BROTHERHOOD

The latest in a long line of Samoan Superstars, the Usos have fought their way to prominence in the Tag Team Division. They are proud of their Polynesian heritage.

SUPERSTAR'S ADVANTAGE

TWIN MAGIC
You see double, and they capitalize

STATS

INTENSITY	7
STRENGTH	4
SPEED	7
COURAGE	6
BRAINS	8

INFO

Height	6'2"/ 6'3"
Weight	220 lbs./ 251 lbs.
From	San Francisco, California
Signature Move	The Samoan Splash
Career Highlights	Sons of WWE Legend Rikishi

THE SHOWDOWN

The match begins at the opening bell, and the Wild Samoans launch into a brutal attack on their younger counterparts. The Usos escape from the ring to strategize, and the referee forces Sika to stand outside the ring at his corner. Jimmy Uso gets back in the ring, and now the match can begin according to the rules.

Wild Samoans

YEARS ACTIVE:	1977–1990

ATTRIBUTES
INTENSITY
UNPREDICTABILITY
BROTHERHOOD

The Wild Samoans are exactly what their name says: wild. They love to attack opponents in unpredictable ways and speak a dialect of Samoan that only they seem to understand.

LEGEND'S ADVANTAGE
WILDNESS
There's a reason they're called the Wild Samoans

STATS

INTENSITY		9
STRENGTH		7
SPEED		7
COURAGE		6
BRAINS		4

INFO

6'2"/ 6'2"	Height
320 lbs./ 319 lbs.	Weight
The Isle of Samoa	From
Samoan Drop; Headbutt	Signature Move
World Tag Team Champions	Career Highlights

3MB (aka the Three Man Band) want to live The Rock 'n' Roll lifestyle. Team captain Heath Slater has long considered himself a rock star, and his partners just want the money, fame, and power that accompany that lifestyle. The Brain Busters have lived that lifestyle since they first joined forces in the 1980s as members of the original Four Horsemen, a powerful group of wrestlers who ruled the '80s.

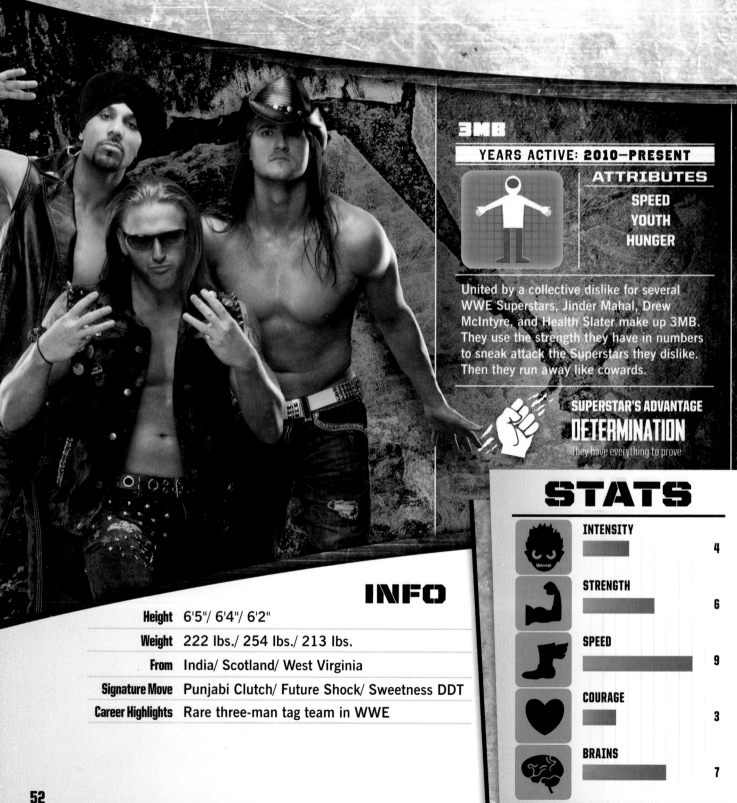

3MB

YEARS ACTIVE: 2010—PRESENT

ATTRIBUTES

SPEED
YOUTH
HUNGER

United by a collective dislike for several WWE Superstars, Jinder Mahal, Drew McIntyre, and Health Slater make up 3MB. They use the strength they have in numbers to sneak attack the Superstars they dislike. Then they run away like cowards.

SUPERSTAR'S ADVANTAGE

DETERMINATION

They have everything to prove

INFO

Height	6'5"/ 6'4"/ 6'2"
Weight	222 lbs./ 254 lbs./ 213 lbs.
From	India/ Scotland/ West Virginia
Signature Move	Punjabi Clutch/ Future Shock/ Sweetness DDT
Career Highlights	Rare three-man tag team in WWE

STATS

	INTENSITY	4
	STRENGTH	6
	SPEED	9
	COURAGE	3
	BRAINS	7

THE SHOWDOWN

The Brain Busters are focused and ready to teach 3MB a lesson about earning what you want. In the ring, Heath Slater begins the match against Arn Anderson. Anderson locks in several submission holds, putting Slater in a lot of pain. Slater is able to tag in his partner Drew McIntyre, but McIntyre feels the pain, too, from Anderson's partner Tully Blanchard.

The Brain Busters

YEARS ACTIVE: 1986–1989

ATTRIBUTES
DRIVE
SMARTS
LOYALTY

First teaming together as original members of the legendary Four Horsemen, Tully Blanchard and Arn Anderson have unequaled ring savvy and drive to be the very best.

LEGEND'S ADVANTAGE

PASSION
No one cares about winning more than these two

STATS

INTENSITY		8
STRENGTH		7
SPEED		7
COURAGE		7
BRAINS		9

INFO

6'1"/ 5'10"	Height
255 lbs./ 225 lbs.	Weight
Minneapolis, Minnesota/ San Antonio, Texas	From
Spinebuster; Piledriver	Signature Move
World Tag Team Champions; NWA Tag Team Champions	Career Highlights

Divas Championship

The newest championship in WWE, the Divas Championship was introduced in 2008. Former *Friday Night SmackDown* General Manager Vickie Guerrero introduced the championship in July of that year. Two years later, the Divas Championship was unified with the WWE's other female championship, the WWE Women's Championship, which was created in 1956. When then-Women's Champion LayCool defeated then-Divas Champion Melina, the Divas division was combined under the Divas Championship, where it has been ever since.

Trish Stratus is considered by many WWE historians to be the greatest WWE Diva of all time, and that makes Eve mad. She thinks she's the best, even if very few others agree. But Eve knows that if she can get in the ring with the best and beat her, she'll own that title. To paraphrase another Legend, "To be the woman, you've got to beat the woman."

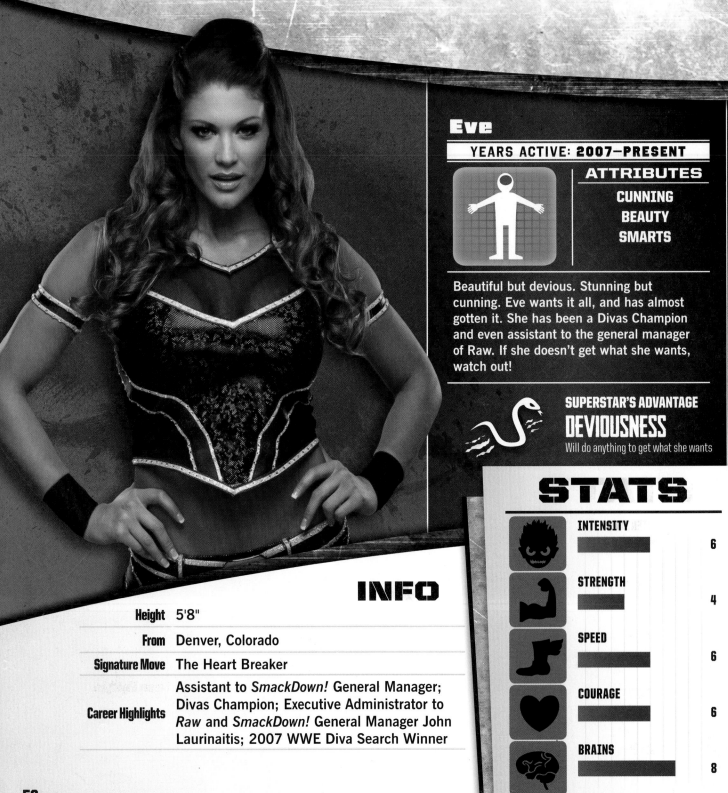

Eve

YEARS ACTIVE: 2007–PRESENT

ATTRIBUTES
CUNNING
BEAUTY
SMARTS

Beautiful but devious. Stunning but cunning. Eve wants it all, and has almost gotten it. She has been a Divas Champion and even assistant to the general manager of Raw. If she doesn't get what she wants, watch out!

SUPERSTAR'S ADVANTAGE
DEVIOUSNESS
Will do anything to get what she wants

STATS

INTENSITY	6
STRENGTH	4
SPEED	6
COURAGE	6
BRAINS	8

INFO

Height	5'8"
From	Denver, Colorado
Signature Move	The Heart Breaker
Career Highlights	Assistant to SmackDown! General Manager; Divas Champion; Executive Administrator to Raw and SmackDown! General Manager John Laurinaitis; 2007 WWE Diva Search Winner

THE SHOWDOWN

Eve is no slouch in the ring, and, though Trish is much more athletic, Eve can fight. She uses a series of elbows to stun Trish before throwing her into the ropes. Eve tries following up with a clothesline, but Trish, a yoga master, arches her back, dodging the move. Trish swings around with a big kick, knocking Eve down.

Trish Stratus

YEARS ACTIVE: 2001–2006

ATTRIBUTES

SPEED
FLEXIBILITY
FEARLESSNESS

Beginning her career as a manager, Trish made the transition to the ring more successfully than any other manager-turned-Superstar. She's also a yoga master, which gives her an athletic edge.

LEGEND'S ADVANTAGE
AGILITY
A yoga teacher, she can move like no one else

STATS

INTENSITY		6
STRENGTH		5
SPEED		8
COURAGE		9
BRAINS		7

INFO

5'4"	**Height**
Toronto, Ontario, Canada	**From**
Stratusfaction; Chick Kick	**Signature Move**
Women's Champion; Hardcore Champion	**Career Highlights**

Other Legends vs. Superstars Matches

Not all Legends were champions during their time in the WWE. But they were still incredibly popular, capturing the excitement and imaginations of the WWE Universe for decades. Some of these, like the Junkyard Dog, would dance with children in the ring, like Brodus Clay does today. Other Legends have enjoyed watching their sons compete in the modern era of WWE, like "The Million Dollar Man" Ted DiBiase, Sr., has done with his son Ted DiBiase. But the WWE Universe has always wondered who would win if these Superstars and Legends faced off in a match.

Let's have a dance off! "Funkasaurus" Brodus Clay and Junkyard Dog are known for their entertaining dance moves. Both competitors even invite children from the WWE Universe into the ring with them to dance after their matches. Even though they like to dance, both are tough competitors in the ring.

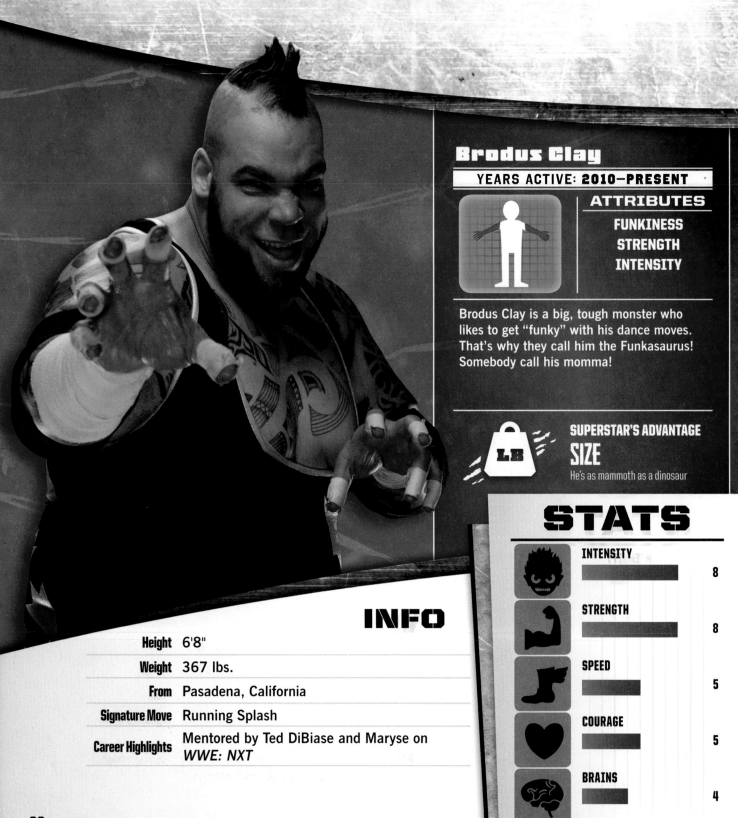

Brodus Clay

YEARS ACTIVE: 2010–PRESENT

ATTRIBUTES

FUNKINESS
STRENGTH
INTENSITY

Brodus Clay is a big, tough monster who likes to get "funky" with his dance moves. That's why they call him the Funkasaurus! Somebody call his momma!

SUPERSTAR'S ADVANTAGE
SIZE
He's as mammoth as a dinosaur

STATS

INTENSITY		8
STRENGTH		8
SPEED		5
COURAGE		5
BRAINS		4

INFO

Height	6'8"
Weight	367 lbs.
From	Pasadena, California
Signature Move	Running Splash
Career Highlights	Mentored by Ted DiBiase and Maryse on *WWE: NXT*

THE SHOWDOWN

The match is slow to begin because, first, Junkyard Dog comes down the aisle to the ring. He struts around the ropes, dancing his way into the ring, and waving to the fans. Then Brodus Clay and his Funkadactyls Naomi and Cameron dance their way in. The crowd cheers as Brodus and JYD stare at each other across mat.

Junkyard Dog

YEARS ACTIVE: 1977–1993

ATTRIBUTES

ATTITUDE
STRENGTH
POPULARITY

A groundbreaking Superstar in the 1970s and '80s, Junkyard Dog was one of the first African American wrestlers to become a national sensation in the wrestling world.

LEGEND'S ADVANTAGE

DETERMINATION

Never gives up

STATS

INTENSITY		4
STRENGTH		8
SPEED		6
COURAGE		9
BRAINS		6

INFO

6'3"	Height
280 lbs.	Weight
Charlotte, North Carolina	From
"Thump" Powerslam	Signature Move
WCW Six-Man Tag Team Champion; Mid-South North American Champion; Mid-South Tag Team Champion	Career Highlights

TED DIBIASE vs.
"MILLION DOLLAR MAN" TED DIBIASE

Generations collide as father and son do battle in WWE. "The Million Dollar Man" Ted DiBiase gave his son Ted DiBiase everything in the world. The younger Ted never had to work for anything in his life. But now junior wants to break out on his own, and the Million Dollar Man is not happy about it. He thinks his son is being ungrateful for rejecting his life of ease.

Ted DiBiase

YEARS ACTIVE: 2008–PRESENT

ATTRIBUTES

HERITAGE
SACRIFICE
TALENT

The son of a WWE Hall of Famer, Ted DiBiase was a member of Legacy with other second- and third-generation Superstars. He's broken out on his own, and away from his father's fortune.

SUPERSTAR'S ADVANTAGE
POSSE
His followers are always nearby

STATS

INTENSITY		7
STRENGTH		7
SPEED		6
COURAGE		7
BRAINS		6

INFO

Height	6'3"
Weight	235 lbs.
From	West Palm Beach, Florida
Signature Move	Dream Street
Career Highlights	World Tag Team Champion; son of WWE Hall of Famer "The Million Dollar Man" Ted DiBiase, Sr.; trained by WWE Hall of Famer Harley Race

THE SHOWDOWN

Both men are hesitant to strike first. Neither one thought they would ever face the other, but it has come to this. Ted Sr. yells at his son, calling him ungrateful. Ted Jr. is insulted and yells back at his father that all he wants to do is move out of his dad's shadow and live on his terms.

Ted DiBiase, Sr.

YEARS ACTIVE: 1975–1994

ATTRIBUTES

WEALTH
SKILLS
INTELLIGENCE

"Million Dollar Man" Ted DiBiase has used his money to buy power and influence in the WWE, including once even buying the WWE Championship. He is also a strong technical wrestler.

LEGEND'S ADVANTAGE
FATHERHOOD
He taught his son and knows his weaknessess

STATS

 INTENSITY 6

 STRENGTH 7

 SPEED 6

 COURAGE 4

 BRAINS 7

INFO

6'1"	Height
260 lbs.	Weight
Palm Beach, Florida	From
Million Dollar Dream	Signature Move
Million Dollar Championship; World Tag Team Champion	Career Highlights

EXPERTS' PICKS

6–7. CM Punk vs. Stone Cold Steve Austin

WINNER: Austin

Punk and Austin continue to fight evenly until Austin, seemingly out of nowhere, slams Punk with the Stone Cold Stunner, allowing Austin to pin and win.

8–9. John Cena vs. Undertaker

WINNER: Undertaker

Despite Cena's warrior heart and tremendous efforts battling against Undertaker's assault, he cannot overpower the man from the dark side. Undertaker buries Cena in the mat with a Tombstone Piledriver for the win.

10–11. The Miz vs. Diesel (aka Kevin Nash)

WINNER: Diesel

The high-speed collision of Miz's face and Diesel's foot resulted in Miz falling down, unconscious. Diesel sets his foot on Miz's chest and scores a pin.

12–13. Alberto Del Rio vs. JBL

WINNER: Alberto Del Rio

Even though JBL had a momentary advantage, Alberto's personal ring announcer Ricardo Rodriguez hits JBL with a chair when the referee isn't looking.

14–15. Brock Lesnar vs. Batista

WINNER: Brock Lesnar

The battle goes back and forth without a clear-cut winner until Lesnar locks Batista in a painful submission. Batista keeps fighting but soon passes out from the searing pain, making Lesnar the winner by default.

18–19. Sheamus vs. The Rock

WINNER: The Rock

Sheamus fights hard, but The Rock relies on his years of experience to surprise Sheamus, first with a Rock Bottom, then a People's Elbow, and finally a pin.

20–21. Big Show vs. Yokozuna

WINNER: Double Count-Out Draw

Yokozuna rolls out of the ring to escape Big Show. Big Show follows, and the two giants battle on the outside, neither hearing the referee count them out of the ring for a 10 count. No one wins.

22–23. Daniel Bryan vs. Booker T

WINNER: Daniel Bryan

With the referee out of it for a minute, Daniel Bryan hits Booker T below the belt and straps on the "No" Lock. The referee gets back to his feet just in time to hear Booker T submit to the painful hold.

24–25. Randy Orton vs. Diamond Dallas Page

WINNER: Randy Orton

Page locks a sleeper hold on Orton, apparently forgetting the signature move he invented could be used from any position. Orton reverses the sleeper hold, hitting DDP with the RKO, proving that the Legend Killer performs the move better.

26–27. Jack Swagger vs. Dusty Rhodes

WINNER: Dusty Rhodes

Swagger poses for the audience and flaunts his superior skills so much that he gets distracted, allowing Rhodes to come at him. Rhodes hits the Bionic Elbow on Swagger's head, knocking him out.

30–31. Kofi Kingston vs. Ricky "The Dragon" Steamboat

WINNER: Ricky "The Dragon" Steamboat

Kofi tries hard, but Steamboat has too much of an experience advantage. Steamboat lands a splash from the top rope and pins the younger Superstar for the win. After the match, Steamboat offers his hand to Kingston, and the teacher shows his respect to the younger man.

32–33. Dolph Ziggler vs. Mr. Perfect

WINNER: Mr. Perfect

The match goes on for nearly an hour with move after move and countermove after countermove. Both men are worn out, but Mr. Perfect musters enough strength to hook Ziggler in a Perfect-Plex and flips him into a pin.

34–35. William Regal vs. "The British Bulldog" Davey Boy Smith

WINNER: William Regal

As the Bulldog moves in for another slam, Regal pulls a pair of brass knuckles from his trunks and, unseen by the referee, knocks out Davey Boy.

36–37. Cody Rhodes vs. Ravishing Rick Rude

WINNER: Cody Rhodes

Rhodes follows up his devastating atomic drop by hitting Rude with the Cross Rhodes, his signature move. Rude can't respond in time and is pinned for the loss.

40–41. Antonio Cesaro vs. "Rowdy" Roddy Piper

WINNER: Roddy Piper

Cesaro may have the talent and the brains, but he lacks experience and tries to outthink Piper. Piper just fights like an animal and defeats his overthinking opponent.

42–43. Zack Ryder vs. Greg Valentine

WINNER: Zack Ryder

Though he's reeling from the Hammer's strikes, Ryder quickly pulls himself together and uses his superior speed to take down Valentine. Ryder hits his signature move, the Rough Ryder, and captures victory. He records his victory celebration on his phone to share with his viewers online.

44–45. Santino Marella vs. "Hacksaw" Jim Duggan

WINNER: Santino Marella

Hacksaw's marching around the ring gives Santino the opportunity to twist his arm and hand into the dreaded Cobra and strike Duggan. Hacksaw falls to the mat, stunned, and Santino steals a pin in under a minute.

48–49. Primo and Epico vs. The Road Warriors

WINNER: The Road Warriors

The first collisions with the Road Warriors prove to be telling for the rest of the match. Hawk and Animal pummel the boys from Puerto Rico and hoist them up into the Doomsday Device. Needless to say, Primo and Epico are finished for this match.

50–51. The Usos vs. The Wild Samoans

WINNERS: The Usos

The Wild Samoans are able to repeatedly strike Jimmy, but when the older Samoans' backs are turned, Jey pulls his brother out of the ring, pretending to be him. He is able to catch the Wild Samoans off guard by "miraculously" returning to health and surprising them with a pin.

52–53. 3MB vs. Brain Busters/Horsemen

WINNERS: Brain Busters

The Brain Busters are, in a word, dominant. They destroy the members of 3MB, hitting them with devastating clotheslines, punches, and their patented Spinebusters. The wannabe rock stars never had a chance against the former Horsemen.

56–57. Eve vs. Trish Stratus

WINNER: Trish Stratus

Trish follows up her big kick with her signature move, Stratusfaction. The match is over before Eve even knows what happened.

60–61. Brodus Clay vs. Junkyard Dog

WINNER: Draw

Brodus Clay and Junkyard Dog stare at each other across the ring…and just start dancing. They invite several children into the ring to join them, and the match is thrown out as a draw.

62–63. Ted DiBiase vs. "Million Dollar Man" Ted DiBiase

WINNER: "Million Dollar Man" Ted DiBiase

Ted Sr. swings an open hand at his son, trying to smack him. Ted Jr. dodges and takes a swing of his own. Ted Sr. ducks that. Ted Jr. backs away and exits the ring. He grabs a ringside microphone and says, "I'm not going to fight you, Dad." Ted Sr. watches in shock as his son walks away from the fight, getting counted out and handing his father a victory.